A Yearlong Guide to Figurative Language

A Yearlong Guide to Figurative Language

8 CONCEPTS TO ENHANCE WRITING

• • •

Includes: Simile, Metaphor, Alliteration, Oxymoron, Onomatopoeia, Hyperbole, Idiom, and Personification

Sean Killeen

Copyright © 2016 Sean Killeen
All rights reserved.

ISBN-13: 9781518646546
ISBN-10: 1518646549

Table of Contents

Alliteration 1
Oxymoron 10
Onomatopoeia 20
Simile 32
Metaphor 44
Personification 59
Hyperbole 69
Idiom 79

A Yearlong Guide to Figurative Language

Name_____ Date _____

Alliteration- the occurrence of the same letter or sound at the beginning of adjacent or closely connected words
1. Alice's aunt Amy ambled across the avenue.
2. Danny danced delightfully during the performance.
3. The tall trees tilted during the storm.
4. Jolly Joan jumped joyfully when she won the prize.

Circle the alliterations listed below, and put ~~a line through~~ sentences that don't contain alliteration.

1. The big, bus buzzed by during the snowstorm.
2. I like to collect baseball cards from every decade.
3. Did Archie really make ten free throws in a row?
4. Sullen Steve silently skated across the pond.
5. Gloria galloped gracefully around the village.
6. Did the sly skunk skillfully spray the predator?
7. Alicia anxiously answered Anita about where she was going.
8. How long did it take Jeff to get to his cottage by the sea?
9. My nervous neighbor nearly jumped five feet when he saw a spider.
10. Will you be going to your appointment?
11. How many times did he do a cartwheel?
12. Mike's meatballs made from scratch are the best around.
13. Shy Shannon shocked the class when she shouted out an answer.
14. The clouded coffee cup is difficult to clean.
15. She types on the computer like Beethoven strokes piano keys.
16. Maynard, Massachusetts is a nice, rural town.
17. Sally's ship sailed across the ocean.
18. The noisy motorcycle raced down the highway.
19. The cool, calm cat crept through the hole in the fence.
20. Jane is an incredible acrobat.

Answer Key

1. The **big, bus buzzed by** during the snowstorm.
2. ~~I like to collect baseball cards from every decade.~~
3. ~~Did Archie really make ten free throws in a row?~~
4. **Sullen Steve silently skated** across the pond.
5. **Gloria galloped gracefully** around the village.
6. Did the **sly skunk skillfully spray** the predator?
7. **Alicia anxiously answered Anita about** where she was going.
8. ~~How long did it take Jeff to get to his cottage by the sea?~~
9. My **nervous neighbor nearly** jumped five feet when he saw a spider.
10. ~~Will you be going to your appointment?~~
11. ~~How many times did he do a cartwheel?~~
12. **Mike's meatballs made** from scratch are the best around.
13. **Shy Shannon shocked** the class when **she shouted** out **an answer**.
14. The **clouded coffee cup** is difficult to clean.
15. ~~She types on the computer like Beethoven strokes piano keys.~~
16. **Maynard, Massachusetts** is a nice, rural town.
17. **Sally's ship sailed** across the ocean.
18. ~~The noisy motorcycle raced down the highway.~~
19. The **cool, calm cat crept** through the hole in the fence.
20. ~~Jane is an incredible acrobat.~~

A Yearlong Guide to Figurative Language

Name_____   Date_____

Please write **true** if alliteration is located in the sentence below and **false** if alliteration is not displayed in the sentence.

1. Paula's parrot pranked the cat.   _____

2. Susie's sister sang all night long.   _____

3. Paul jumped up and down after the commencement.   _____

4. Is an aardvark an ordinary mammal?   _____

5. Why do all my kites get caught in the wires above?   _____

6. Is it possible to swim across the Atlantic Ocean?   _____

7. The tall tree swayed back and forth during the storm.   _____

8. Betty's best buddy built a barn house in one week.   _____

9. The cracked phone fell under the bed.   _____

10. The jolly jack-o-lantern just fell over.   _____

11. My friend found fifty dollars at the beach.   _____

12. I am running out of olives so I need to get some more.   _____

13. What is your favorite number?   _____

14. Is it impossible to have a dream come true?   _____

15. The ancient antique artifact is worth a million dollars.   _____

16. I went shopping last week for a new car.   _____

17. Wild winds pushed the clouds across the sky.   _____

18. My pencil keeps breaking whenever I write my answers.   _____

19. How many states have two or less borders?   _____

20. How many people are in your family?   _____

Answer Key

1. Paula's parrot pranked the cat. **True**
2. Susie's sister sang all night long. **True**
3. Paul jumped up and down after the commencement. **False**
4. Is an aardvark and ordinary mammal? **True**
5. Why do all my kites get caught in the wires above? **False**
6. Is it possible to swim across the Atlantic Ocean? **False**
7. The tall tree swayed back and forth during the storm. **True**
8. Betty's best buddy built a barn house in one week. **True**
9. The cracked phone fell under the bed. **False**
10. The jolly jack-o-lantern just fell over. **True**
11. My friend found fifty dollars at the beach. **True**
12. I am running out of olives, so I need to get more. **True**
13. What is your favorite number? **False**
14. Is it impossible to have a dream come true? **True**
15. The ancient antique artifact is worth a million dollars. **True**
16. I went shopping last week for a new car. **False**
17. Wild winds pushed the clouds across the sky. **True**
18. My pencil keeps breaking when I write my answers. **False**
19. How many states have two or less borders? **False**
20. How many people are in your family? **False**

Name _____ Date_____

ate apples	cat clawed	icy igloo	cranky cricket	high heels
white wallet	jaguar jumped	beagle barked	eager elephant	quivering quail
big bears	took tools	Tommy's tux	seven sisters	frigid face
eats eggs	lazy lion	brown bunny	tall table	bouncy ball

1. Kristine wore _____ to the ball.
2. My _____ the couch and now there are holes everywhere.
3. The _____ chirped all night long, but we couldn't find him.
4. John _____ every morning for breakfast.
5. Bonnie's _____ hopped down the trail.
6. The _____ bumped into the wall.
7. The horse _____ as a treat for the day.
8. The _____ slept in its nest.
9. The _____ guided the herd across the African plains.
10. Tim's _____ was as red as a beet from the cold.
11. Leo the _____ napped all day long.
12. That sure is a _____ for the infant to reach.
13. While I was in the rain forest, a _____ into a river.
14. Mr. Whipple's _____ at the trespassers.
15. The carpenter _____ to his building site.
16. The _____ laughed all night about childhood memories.
17. _____ was spotless as he gave his speech.
18. If you go to Kodiak Island, you will see some _____ .
19. I ventured to Siberia and slept in an _____ .
20. My _____ has been missing for days and I have no money.

Answer Key

1. Kristine wore **high heels** to the ball.
2. My **cat clawed** the couch and now there are holes everywhere.
3. The **cranky cricket** chirped all night long, but nobody could find him.
4. John **eats eggs** every morning for breakfast.
5. Bonnie's **brown bunny** hopped down the trail.
6. The **bouncy ball** bumped into the wall.
7. The horse **ate apples** as a treat for the day.
8. The **quivering quail** slept in his nest.
9. The **eager elephant** guided the herd across the African plains.
10. Tim's **frigid face** was as red as a beet from the cold.
11. Leo the **lazy lion** napped all day long.
12. That sure is a **tall table** for the infant to reach.
13. While I was in the rain forest, a **jaguar jumped** into a river.
14. Mr. Whipple's **beagle barked** at the trespassers.
15. The carpenter **took tools** to his building site.
16. The **seven sisters** laughed all night about childhood memories.
17. **Tommy's tuxedo** was spotless as he gave his speech.
18. If you go to Kodiak Island, you will see some **big bears**.
19. I ventured to Siberia and slept in an **icy igloo**.
20. My **white wallet** has been missing for days and I have no money.

Name_____ Date _____

Please use the following alliteration examples in sentences.

1. (dazzling Darlene danced delightfully)

   _____

2. (happy Henry hopped)

   _____

3. (agitated alligator ambled)

   _____

4. (big, brown bear bounced)

   _____

5. (sappy sugar slid)

   _____

6. (calm cat clawed)

   _____

7. (ice cream is interesting)

   _____

8. (old, outgoing owl)

   _____

9. (Will winked wildly)

   _____

10. (Ryan ran rapidly)

    _____

Name_____ Date _____

Please write a comprehensive paragraph using at least four alliteration examples.

Name_____ Date _____

Please use an example of alliteration in a complete sentence. Make an illustration of your alliteration example.

Name_____   Date _____

> **Oxymoron-** conjoining contradictory terms
> **Examples:**
> 1. Your only choice is to listen the first time.
> 2. May I have the larger half please?
> 3. I am a definite maybe for the party.
> 4. Where is the original copy?

Circle the oxymoron examples listed below, and ~~put a line~~ through sentences that do not contain an oxymoron.

1. Please provide us with an opinion.
2. The jumbo shrimp comes with a salad.
3. The plastic glasses are for the social event.
4. My dad came to a rolling stop last week.
5. That was one funny play.
6. It's the same difference whenever you travel.
7. I like to run marathons at a fast pace.
8. Friday is a working holiday.
9. My cousin burnt the chicken.
10. Isn't the flower growing?
11. How far can you run in ten minutes?
12. Please act naturally and be yourself when the boss is here.
13. My wallet was found missing last week.
14. There was a deafening silence when the tiger paced in his cage.
15. May I have the larger half of the pizza?
16. Please tell me you won the game.
17. My Aunt Millie is the funniest person I know.
18. I am a definite maybe for attending the ball.
19. Are we alone together with our answer?
20. George shuffled across the stage rather quietly.

Answer Key

1. ~~Please provide us with an opinion.~~
2. The **jumbo shrimp** comes with a salad.
3. The **plastic glasses** are for the social event.
4. My dad came to a **rolling stop** last week.
5. ~~That was one funny play.~~
6. It's the **same difference** whenever you travel.
7. I like to run marathons at a **fast pace**.
8. Friday is a **working holiday**.
9. ~~My cousin burnt the chicken.~~
10. ~~Isn't the flower growing?~~
11. ~~How far can you run in ten minutes?~~
12. Please **act naturally** and be yourself when the boss is here.
13. My wallet was **found missing** last week.
14. There was a **deafening silence** when the tiger paced in his cage.
15. May I have the **larger half** of the pizza?
16. ~~Please tell me you won the game.~~
17. ~~My Aunt Millie is the funniest person I know.~~
18. I am a **definite maybe** for attending the ball.
19. Are we **alone together** with our answer?
20. ~~George shuffled across the stage rather quickly.~~

Name_____ Date _____

Please write **true** if an oxymoron is located in the sentence below or **false** if an oxymoron does not exist.

1. Good grief I missed my exit again! _____

2. That was a pretty ugly fall he took off his bike. _____

3. That is almost exactly what I was thinking. _____

4. The waterfall is the most amazing I have ever seen. _____

5. Please place the plastic glasses on the dinner table. _____

6. I would love to see the whole world laughing. _____

7. That is a genuine imitation of my stockings. _____

8. I forgot about my peas and now they are freezer burnt. _____

9. Your only choice is to go to the airport to pick up your uncle. _____

10. I am going to take it easy today. _____

11. It is the same difference if you take Oak Street or Elm Ave. _____

12. Which current states were colonies in America? _____

13. Africa is such a beautiful continent. _____

14. There was a silent scream in the theater. _____

15. I am not worried because it's a minor crisis. _____

16. John came to a rolling stop on his bicycle. _____

17. Have you ever been to an amusement park at night? _____

18. The Great Depression was a very sad period in time. _____

19. I ate a sweet tart and now my mouth feels funny. _____

20. The highway runs through town for a few miles. _____

Answer Key

1. **Good grief**, I missed my exit again! — **True**
2. That was a **pretty ugly** fall he took off his bike. — **True**
3. That is **almost exactly** what I was thinking. — **True**
4. The waterfall is the most amazing I have ever seen. — **False**
5. Please place the **plastic glasses** on the dinner table. — **True**
6. I would love to see the whole world laughing. — **False**
7. That is a **genuine imitation** of my stockings. — **True**
8. I forgot about my peas and now they are **freezer burnt**. — **True**
9. Your **only choice** is to go to the airport to pick up your uncle. — **True**
10. I am going to take it easy today. — **False**
11. It is the **same difference** if you take Oak Street or Elm Ave. — **True**
12. Which current states were colonies in America? — **False**
13. Africa is such a beautiful continent. — **False**
14. There was a **silent scream** in the theater. — **True**
15. I am not worried because it's a **minor crisis**. — **True**
16. John came to a **rolling stop** on his bicycle. — **True**
17. Have you ever been to an amusement park at night? — **False**
18. The **Great Depression** was a very sad period of time. — **True**
19. I ate a **sweet tart** and now my mouth feels funny, — **True**
20. The highway runs through town for a few miles. — **False**

Name_____   Date _____

Fill in the blank.

fake plant	near miss	old news	nervously relaxed	student teacher
a fine mess	little big	almost candid	brief speech	artificial grass
anxious patient	small giraffe	fuzzy logic	bad luck	bittersweet
dark star	fast snail	awfully nice	cowardly lion	dry creek

1. The _____ hid behind the bush.
2. The football game will be played on_____ .
3. Our class will be getting a very nice_____ next semester.
4. The horse approached the_____ looking for water.
5. Did you see the_____ during the full moon?
6. You've gotten yourself into a_____
7. The_____ ambled across the grass.
8. That was_____ of you to bring flowers.
9. The_____ beat the ant in a race.
10. She gave us_____ that we already knew about.
11. The news anchor said there was a_____ at the airport.
12. It was a_____ victory for the home team.
13. If it weren't for_____ I wouldn't have any.
14. The _____ rumbled through the forest.
15. I thought the governor was going to give a _____
16. The_____ paced in the waiting room for hours.
17. There is some_____ behind that theory.
18. You were_____ during the snapshot.
19. Aren't you a_____ to be doing cartwheels?
20. I feel_____ for my presentation.

Answer Key

1. The **fake plant** hid behind the bush.
2. The football game will be played on **artificial grass**.
3. Our class will be getting a very nice **student teacher** next semester.
4. The horse approached the **dry creek** looking for water.
5. Did you see the **dark star** during the full moon?
6. You've gotten yourself into a **fine mess**.
7. The **small giraffe** ambled across the grass.
8. That was **awfully nice** of you to bring flowers.
9. The **fast snail** beat the ant in a race.
10. She gave us **old news** that we already knew about.
11. The news anchor said there was a **near miss** at the airport.
12. It was a **bittersweet** victory for the home team.
13. If it weren't for **bad luck** I wouldn't have any.
14. The **cowardly lion** rumbled through the forest.
15. I thought the governor was going to give a **brief speech**.
16. The **anxious patient** paced in the waiting room for hours.
17. There is some **fuzzy logic** behind that theory.
18. You were **almost candid** during the snapshot.
19. Aren't you a **little big** to be doing cartwheels?
20. I feel **nervously relaxed** for my presentation.

Name _____ Date _____

Please use the following oxymoron examples in sentences.

1. (deafening silence) _____
_____

2. (almost exact) _____
_____

3. (exact estimate) _____
_____

4. (liquid gas) _____
_____

5. (minor crisis) _____
_____

6. (clearly confused) _____
_____

7. (hot chili) _____
_____

8. (taped live) _____
_____

9. (same difference) _____
_____

10. (seriously funny) _____
_____

Name_____ Date _____

What does each oxymoron example mean?

Example: My grandmother always says you will not get hurt eating clean dirt.
No dirt is really clean, but in the end it can't really hurt you.

1. I slept on a hard pillow all night long.

_____

2. I feel all alone today.

_____

3. If you use invisible ink I won't be able to read what you wrote.

_____

4. The plane is approaching at a low altitude.

_____

5. Who has a mean smile on their face today?

_____

6. Oh my, that is such old news!

_____

7. Please turn off the dim light when you leave the room.

_____

8. Wasn't that such a quiet storm that passed through town?

_____

9. My cousin Al lives on the top floor of his apartment complex.

_____

10. I'm half full from that meal.

_____

Name_____ Date _____

Please write a comprehensive paragraph using at least four oxymoron examples.

Name_____ Date _____

Please write a sentence using an oxymoron. Illustrate your oxymoron sentence.

Name_____   Date _____

> **Onomatopoeia:** the use of a word to describe or imitate a natural sound or the sound made by an object or action
>
> **Examples:**
> 1. The <u>woof</u> from the puppy made me jump in the air.
> 2. The snake scared me with a <u>hiss</u>.
> 3. The balloon broke with a loud <u>pop</u>.
> 4. The table went <u>boom</u> and broke when I leaned against it.

(Circle) the **onomatopoeia** examples listed below, and put ~~a line through~~ sentences that do not contain **onomatopoeia**.

1. Did you hear the birds this morning?
2. The engine went *vroom* as the racers rounded the corner.
3. My shoes went *flip-flop* in the puddles.
4. We take dance lessons.
5. I like to go to the music store and listen to new songs.
6. The ink fell on John's story.
7. Tom drinks water way too quickly for attention.
8. *Ding-dong* went the bell to signal the end of the day.
9. The door opened with a *creak*.
10. The cup fell to the floor with a *clatter*.
11. *Cock-a-doodle-doo*, crowed the rooster.
12. The clock is always wrong.
13. The cow wants to be fed quite soon.
14. Fireworks burst in the sky with a loud *boom*.
15. The duck swam in the pond.
16. Her heels landed on the floor with a *clack* as she walked.
17. The birds like to *tweet-tweet* outside my window.
18. Don't talk so loudly.
19. I was so cold my hands froze.
20. I heard the *clang* of the falling items.

Answer Key

1. ~~Did you hear the birds this morning?~~
2. The engine went **vroom** as the racers rounded the corner.
3. My shoes went ***flip-flop*** in the puddles.
4. ~~We take dance lessons.~~
5. ~~I like to go to the music store and listen to new songs.~~
6. ~~The ink fell on John's story.~~
7. ~~Tom drinks water way too quickly for attention.~~
8. ***Ding-dong*** went the bell to signal the end of the day.
9. The door opened with a ***creak***.
10. The cup fell to the floor with a ***clatter***.
11. **Cock-a-doodle-doo**, crowed the rooster.
12. ~~The clock is always wrong.~~
13. ~~The cow wants to be fed quite soon.~~
14. Fireworks burst in the sky with a loud ***boom***.
15. ~~The duck *swam in the pond*.~~
16. Her heels landed on the floor with a ***clack*** as she walked.
17. The birds like to **tweet-tweet** outside my window.
18. ~~Don't *talk* so loudly.~~
19. ~~I was so cold my hands froze.~~
20. I heard the ***clang*** of the falling items.

Name_____ Date _____

Please write **true** if an onomatopoeia example is located in the sentence below or **false** if onomatopoeia does not exist.

1. The sheep made a *baa* sound in the field. _____

2. *Boom* went the thunder as the storm rolled along. _____

3. The butterfly is an amazing sight. _____

4. I went to the zoo and I saw so many cool animals. _____

5. The basketball *swished* as it fell into the net. _____

6. The alarm has been going off all day long. _____

7. My friend Luis is driving in the rain. _____

8. *Ding-dong* the bell sounded and made me jump ten feet. _____

9. Please call a plumber as the *drip* from the faucet is causing water damage. _____

10. What is your address so I can mail you a letter? _____

11. Will the department store be open over the weekend? _____

12. *Vroom* the engine roared as it traveled down the highway. _____

13. The moth will soon move its wings and fly away. _____

14. I have to get the decorations from the attic. _____

15. The *thud* of the tree falling made everybody jump. _____

16. May I please call my mother to see if I can eat dinner here? _____

17. The water went *swoosh* as it flowed down the drain. _____

18. Mike and Tommy will be taking supplies to the shed. _____

19. The *crinkle* of the leaves reminded me it was autumn. _____

20. The toilet flushed with a *whoosh* of water. _____

Answer Key

1. The sheep made a **baa** sound in the field. — **True**
2. **Boom** went the thunder as the storm rolled along. — **True**
3. The butterfly is an amazing sight. — **False**
4. I went to the zoo and I saw so many cool animals. — **False**
5. The basketball **swished** as it fell into the net. — **True**
6. The alarm has been going off all day long. — **False**
7. My friend Luis is driving in the rain. — **False**
8. **Ding-dong** the bell sounded and made me jump ten feet. — **True**
9. Please call a plumber as the **drip** from the faucet is causing water damage. — **True**
10. What is your address so I can mail you a letter? — **False**
11. Will the department store be open over the weekend? — **False**
12. **Vroom** the engine roared as it traveled down the highway. — **True**
13. The moth will soon move its wings and fly away. — **False**
14. I have to get the decorations from the attic. — **False**
15. The **thud** of the tree falling made everybody jump. — **True**
16. May I please call my mother to see if I can eat dinner here? — **False**
17. The water went **swoosh** as it flowed down the drain. — **True**
18. Mike and Tommy will be taking supplies to the shed. — **False**
19. The **crinkle** of the leaves reminded me it was autumn. — **True**
20. The toilet flushed with a **whoosh** of water. — **True**

Name_____ **Date**_____

Fill in the blank.

crunch	clink	sniff	plop	bump
purr	ding	pop	choo-choo	roar
baa	screech	crackle	vroom	whoop
moo	snap	boom	honk	squeal

1. The horn rang with a _____.
2. The glasses slammed together with a _____.
3. I love to _____ a nice smelling batch of cookies.
4. The pig chased the chicken around the barn with a loud _____.
5. I don't like when people eat their cereal with a _____.
6. _____, wailed the sheep.
7. She kept the steady beat of the music with a _____ of her fingers.
8. His head hit the wall with a sickening _____.
9. The fireworks on the Fourth of July made a loud _____!
10. The fastball slid into the catcher's mitt with a _____.
11. The cow's _____ was quiet.
12. My cat snuggles on the couch with a soft _____.
13. The lion filled the air with a fierce _____.
14. I get nervous when the train makes the _____ sound.
15. The tires went _____ as he tried to put on the brakes.
16. _____! The fireplace lit up the room.
17. _____ went the bell as it fell on the floor.
18. He let out a loud _____ at the graduation ceremony.
19. The _____ of the engine could be heard around town.
20. The _____ from the rain made the farmer smile.

Answer Key

1. The horn rang with a **honk**.
2. The glasses slammed together with a **clink**.
3. I love to **sniff** a nice smelling batch of cookies.
4. The pig chased the chicken around the barn with a loud **squeal**.
5. I don't like when people eat their cereal with a **crunch**.
6. **Baa**, wailed the sheep.
7. She kept the steady beat of the music with a **snap** of her fingers.
8. His head hit the wall with a sickening **bump**.
9. The fireworks on the Fourth of July made a loud **boom**!
10. The fastball slid into the catcher's mitt with a **pop**.
11. The cow's **moo** was quiet.
12. My cat snuggles on the couch with a soft **purr**.
13. The lion filled the air with a fierce **roar**.
14. I get nervous when the train makes the **choo-choo** sound.
15. The tires went **screech** as he tried to put on the brakes.
16. **Crackle**! The fireplace lit up the room.
17. **Ding** went the bell as it fell on the floor.
18. He let out a loud **whoop** at the graduation ceremony.
19. The **vroom** of the engine could be heard around town.
20. The **plop** from the rain made the farmer smile.

Name_____ Date _____

Please use the following onomatopoeia samples in sentences

1. (click) _____
_____

2. (chirp) _____
_____

3. (puff) _____
_____

4. (purr) _____
_____

5. (fizz) _____
_____

6. (meow) _____
_____

7. (knock) _____
_____

8. (moo) _____
_____

9. (clatter) _____
_____

10. (boom) _____
_____

Name_____ Date _____

What does each onomatopoeia example mean?
Example: Moo! The cow called for more hay.
   The cow made a noise.

1. *Hoot!* The owl could be heard in the forest.

   _____

2. The *crackle* of the popcorn cooking reminds me of a movie house.

   _____

3. My mom made bacon and the *sizzle* was amazing.

   _____

4. *Poof!* The clouds disappeared.

   _____

5. The *whiz* of the plane frightened the child.

   _____

6. The *knock* on the door told me a visitor was at my home.

   _____

7. *Bang!* The fireworks brightened the sky.

   _____

8. The *swoosh* of the water overflowed from the sink.

   _____

9. *Plop!* The drips from the storm fell to the ground.

   _____

10. *Snap! Crackle! Pop!* I can't wait to eat this cereal.

    _____

Name _____ Date _____

Please write a comprehensive paragraph using at least four examples of onomatopoeia.

Name _____ Date _____

Please write a sentence using an example of onomatopoeia. Illustrate that example.

Name_____ Date _____

Please circle the correct response.

1. The *buzz* in the crowd was so amazing.
   oxymoron   onomatopoeia   other

2. Will you be going to your appointment later in the month?
   oxymoron   onomatopoeia   other

3. My cousin freezer burnt the chicken for the fifth time this year.
   oxymoron   onomatopoeia   other

4. Isn't the flower taking forever to grow?
   oxymoron   onomatopoeia   other

5. Please act naturally and be yourself when the boss is here.
   oxymoron   onomatopoeia   other

6. My wallet was found missing near the library last week.
   oxymoron   onomatopoeia   other

7. *Cock-a-doodle-doo*, crowed the rooster.
   oxymoron   onomatopoeia   other

8. There was a deafening silence when the tiger paced in his cage.
   oxymoron   onomatopoeia   other

9. The clock goes *tick-tock* all day long.
   oxymoron   onomatopoeia   other

10. The *pop* of the fireworks made my ears ring for minutes.
    oxymoron   onomatopoeia   other

ANSWER KEY

Answers have been marked in bold.

1. The *buzz* in the crowd was so amazing.
   oxymoron   **onompatopeia**   other

2. Will you be going to your appointment later in the month?
   oxymoron   onomatopoeia   **other**

3. My cousin freezer burnt the chicken for the fifth time this year.
   oxymoron   onomatopoeia   other

4. Isn't the flower taking forever to grow?
   oxymoron   onomatopoeia   **other**

5. Please act naturally and be yourself when the boss is here.
   oxymoron   onomatopoeia   other

6. My wallet was found missing near the library last week.
   oxymoron   onomatopoeia   other

7. *Cock-a-doodle-doo*, crowed the rooster.
   oxymoron   **onomatopoeia**   other

8. There was a deafening silence when the tiger paced in his cage.
   oxymoron   onomatopoeia   other

9. The clock goes *tick-tock* all day long.
   oxymoron   **onomatopoeia**   other

10. The *pop* of the fireworks made my ears ring for minutes.
    oxymoron   **onomatopoeia**   other

Name_____   Date _____

Simile- a comparison that uses the words like or as **Examples:**
1. It is as hot as an oven in here.
2. Phillip laughed like a clown after hearing the ridiculous story.
3. Brad is as tall as a tree in his class.
4. Miss Kim's heart is as big as an elephant.

Circle the similes listed below, and put a line through sentences that don't contain a simile.

1. Maria likes to paint pictures of the blue skies.
2. Harry was as happy as a lark when he found his wallet.
3. Kelly is as hungry as a bear and needs some food.
4. Joe is like a fish in the water when he swims laps.
5. CJ ran like the wind during the race.
6. Mrs. Myers is an amazing cook.
7. Tom made thirty-three cupcakes as fast as lightning.
8. Missy is as smart as an encyclopedia with world geography.
9. I like to ride my bike after school.
10. Tara can talk as quickly as an auctioneer when she is excited.
11. Is Danny in the first grade?
12. My neighbor likes running around the track for miles on end.
13. She had goose bumps the size of softballs after meeting her favorite actress.
14. It was as hot as the sun outside during recess today.
15. Alice is as angry as a hornet after losing her money.
16. Timmy likes going to farms and petting the animals.
17. The county fair is as big as an ocean.
18. It's raining buckets today, and I wanted to have a picnic.
19. She likes traveling to countries far away.
20. Mollie picks up trash like a vacuum cleaner picks up dust.

Answer Key

1. ~~Maria likes to paint pictures of the blue skies.~~
2. Harry was as happy as a lark when he found his wallet.
3. Kelly is as hungry as a bear and needs some food.
4. Joe is like a fish in the water when he swims laps.
5. CJ ran like the wind during the race.
6. ~~Mrs. Myers is an amazing cook.~~
7. Tom made thirty-three cupcakes as fast as lightning.
8. Missy is as smart as an encyclopedia with world geography.
9. ~~I like to ride my bike after school.~~
10. Tara can talk as quickly as an auctioneer when she is excited.
11. ~~Is Danny in the first grade?~~
12. ~~My neighbor likes running around the track for miles on end.~~
13. ~~She had goose bumps the size of softballs after meeting her favorite actress.~~
14. It was as hot as the sun outside during recess today.
15. Alice is as angry as a hornet after losing her money.
16. ~~Timmy likes going to farms and petting the animals.~~
17. The county fair is as big as an ocean.
18. ~~It's raining buckets today, and I wanted to have a picnic.~~
19. ~~She likes traveling to countries far away.~~
20. Mollie picks up trash like a vacuum cleaner picks up dust.

Name_____   Date _____

Please write **true** if a simile is located in the sentence below or **false** if a simile is not listed.

1. I really like deep-sea fishing with friends. _____

2. Can you smile like a cat? _____

3. Shannon is such a funny person. _____

4. Bobby can swim like a dolphin while in the pool. _____

5. Tyrell is a redwood of a man. _____

6. Missy is as calm as a clam when she is on stage. _____

7. The campground is as open as a prairie with all its land. _____

8. My hat fell off my head when I ran up the hill. _____

9. Eleanor is as bright as the sun when she answers difficult problems. _____

10. Tracy is as quiet as a mouse while studying for her exams. _____

11. Wendy likes the Los Angeles Dodgers. _____

12. Christy is as excited as a puppy when her team wins big games. _____

13. The girls on the track team can sprint really fast. _____

14. My friend knows so much about volcanoes. _____

15. Michael can be as sharp as a tack when he recites poetry. _____

16. Are the dogs really running as quietly as the wind? _____

17. Kylie like monkeys more than anything. _____

18. Who can laugh like a hyena? _____

19. My family likes taking long trips to New England. _____

20. Mrs. Jones's rabbit is as clever as fox when it comes to finding food. _____

Answer Key

1. I really like deep-sea fishing with friends. **False**
2. Can you smile like a cat? **True**
3. Shannon is such a funny person. **False**
4. Bobby can swim like a dolphin while in the pool. **True**
5. Tyrell is a redwood of a man. **False**
6. Missy is as calm as a clam when she is on stage. **True**
7. The campground is as open as a prairie with all its land. **True**
8. My hat fell off my head when I ran up the hill. **False**
9. Eleanor is as bright as the sun when she answers difficult problems. **True**
10. Tracy is as quiet as a mouse while studying for her exams. **True**
11. Wendy likes the Los Angeles Dodgers. **False**
12. Christy is as excited as a puppy when her team wins big games. **True**
13. The girls on the track team can sprint really fast. **False**
14. My friend knows so much about volcanoes. **False**
15. Michael can be as sharp as a tack when he recites poetry. **True**
16. Are the dogs really running as quietly as the wind? **True**
17. Kylie like monkeys more than anything. **False**
18. Who can laugh like a hyena? **True**
19. My family likes taking long trips to New England. **False**
20. Mrs. Jones's rabbit is as clever as fox when it comes to finding food. **True**

Name_____ Date _____

Fill in the blank.

as tall as a tree	as loud as a trumpet	like a roller coaster	as pretty as a flower
as quiet as a mouse	like the wind	like a monkey	like a fish
as funny as a clown	as smart as a computer	like a dream	like a rose
like a volcano	as wise as an owl	as cold as ice	like a garbage dump
as blind as a bat	like spaghetti	as smooth as glass	as shiny as a star

1. The first place winner in the 100-yard dash ran_____.
2. Millie is_____ when she climbs trees.
3. Mr. Larkin is_____ with his jokes.
4. The girl's voice is _____.
5. My dad is_____ when it comes to algebra.
6. Pauline can swim_____ in the ocean.
7. While I was studying in the library, it was_____.
8. My stomach feels_____ due to the oral report.
9. Joseph is_____, and he is still growing.
10. The dress is_____.
11. The roads wrapped around the mountain_____.
12. The umpire must be_____ after that call.
13. John will explode_____ when he finds out his goldfish is sick.
14. The pizza is _____.
15. My grandmother is_____ with her memory.
16. His room is_____.
17. Her diamond ring is_____.
18. The calm lake is_____ today.
19. Jimmy's teacher says he is_____ due to his amazing attitude.
20. The room smelled_____ after it was cleaned.

Answer Key

1. The first place winner in the 100-yard dash ran **like the wind.**
2. Millie is **like a monkey** when she climbs trees.
3. Mr. Larkin is **as funny as a clown** with his jokes.
4. The girl's voice is **as loud as a trumpet,** and I need to cover my ears.
5. My dad is **as smart as a computer** when it comes to algebra.
6. Pauline can swim **like a fish** in the ocean.
7. While I was studying in the library, it was **as quiet as a mouse.**
8. My stomach feels **like a roller coaster** due to the oral report.
9. Joseph is **as tall as a tree**, and he is still growing.
10. The dress is **as pretty as a flower**.
11. The roads wrapped around the mountain **like spaghetti**.
12. The umpire must be **as blind as a bat** after that call.
13. John will explode **like a volcano** when he finds out his goldfish is sick.
14. The pizza is **as cold as ice**.
15. My grandmother is **as wise as an owl** with her memory.
16. His room is **like a garbage dump**.
17. Her diamond ring is **as shiny as a star**.
18. The calm lake is **as smooth as glass** today.
19. Jimmy's teacher says he is **like a dream** due to his amazing attitude.
20. The room smelled **like a rose** after it was cleaned.

Name _____ Date _____

Please fill in the blank spaces to make the similes complete sentences.
Examples:

My _____ is as tall as a/an _____ .

My **sister** is as tall as a **building**.

Missy is like a/an _____ when she swims.

Missy is like a **dolphin** when she swims.

1. The puppy is as _____ as a/an _____ .

2. Mr. Tom is as _____ as a/an _____ .

3. The fox is as _____ as a/an _____ .

4. Amy can do a flip as _____ .

5. I am running like _____ .

6. The turtle is crawling like _____ .

7. The mouse is like _____ .

8. Jimmy's parrot is as _____ .

9. The owl is as smart as _____ .

10. Kent can jump like _____ .

Please write your own similes in complete sentences.

1. _____

2. _____

3. _____

4. _____

5. _____

Name_____ Date _____

Example: (like a baker) <u>My brother can bake cookies like a baker.</u>
Use the following similes in sentences.

1. (as soft as a pillow) _____
   _____

2. (as tall as a tree) _____
   _____

3. (like a rocket) _____
   _____

4. (like the wind) _____
   _____

5. (as sharp as a tack) _____
   _____

6. (as busy as a beaver) _____
   _____

7. (like a kangaroo) _____
   _____

8. (like an acrobat) _____
   _____

9. (like coal) _____
   _____

10. (as white as clouds) _____
    _____

Name _____ Date _____

What does each simile example mean?
Example: Pauline's red hair is as beautiful as a sunset.
         This simile means Pauline has really pretty red hair.

1. Mrs. Knight can sing like a bird in her church choir.

   _____

2. Mr. Chung cut through the logs like a beaver to a twig.

   _____

3. Shea is as funny as a jester.

   _____

4. Mariah is as tall as a skyscraper.

   _____

5. I am like a porcupine in a balloon shop.

   _____

6. My cousin is as bald as an eagle.

   _____

7. My sister's bathroom is as neat as a squeaky clean whistle.

   _____

8. Zina was as proud as a peacock when she received an A on her state report.

   _____

9. Mr. Apple is as poor as a pauper, but he has the best attitude in the world.

   _____

10. My friend Kent is as strong as a bull.

    _____

Answer Key

Answers are open for interpretation.

1. Mrs. Knight can sing like a bird in her church choir.
   Mrs. Knight has a nice voice.

2. Mr. Chung cut through the logs like a beaver to a twig.
   He is good at cutting logs. He works like a lumberjack.

3. Shea is as funny as a jester.
   Shea has a good sense of humor.

4. Mariah is as tall as a skyscraper.
   Mariah's height is above average.

5. I am like a porcupine in a balloon shop.
   I am clumsy.

6. My cousin is as bald as an eagle.
   My cousin doesn't have any hair.

7. My sister's bathroom is as neat as a squeaky clean whistle.
   My sister's room is clean.

8. Zina was as proud as a peacock when she received an A on her state report.
   Zina was excited she did well.

9. Mr. Apple is as poor as a pauper, but he has the best attitude in the world.
   Mr. Apple might not have a lot of money, but he is a kind person.

10. My friend Kent is as strong as a bull.
    Kent is a strong person.

Name_____ Date _____

Please write a comprehensive paragraph using at least four similes.

Name_____ Date _____

Please write a sentence using a favorite simile. Illustrate that favorite simile.

Name_____   Date _____

> **Metaphor-** compares two things without using like or as and uses a word or phrase that means one thing to describe another.
> **Examples:**
> 1. **Brittany is a princess** with her grace.
> 2. His **Grand Canyon smile** brightens the day.
> 3. Henry is a **jukebox with his music** knowledge.
> 4. Michael is a **clown with his jokes**.

(Circle) the metaphors listed below, and put ~~a line through~~ sentences which don't contain a metaphor.

1. Brenda is a redwood with her height.
2. Rachel is smart in our class.
3. Eleanor can count really fast.
4. Erin is a statue when she stands still.
5. I was a rock last night when I slept.
6. That math test was a breeze to me.
7. Jill is the class historian with social studies.
8. She is a rainbow with her outgoing personality.
9. Nancy is a butterfly when she is on stage doing ballet.
10. Maria dances to salsa music every Saturday night.
11. Amy can smile like a Cheshire cat when she is happy.
12. Did Sally really act like a robot at the dance?
13. The mayor wears many different hats in his job.
14. Please table the party until next week.
15. Mike is a Rolodex with his filing system.
16. She is a clock when it comes to telling time.
17. Ireland is a country in Europe.
18. Frank is a surgeon with his precision.
19. Mary walked like a soldier down the hall.
20. Ciaran is a king with his riches.

Answer Key

1. Brenda is a redwood with her height.
2. ~~Rachel is smart in our class.~~
3. ~~Eleanor can count really fast.~~
4. Erin is a statue when she stands still.
5. I was a rock last night when I slept.
6. ~~That math test was a breeze to me.~~
7. Jill is the class historian with social studies.
8. She is a rainbow with her outgoing personality.
9. Nancy is a butterfly when she is on stage doing ballet.
10. ~~Maria dances to salsa music every Saturday night.~~
11. ~~Amy can smile like a Cheshire cat when she is happy.~~
12. ~~Did Sally really act like a robot at the dance?~~
13. The mayor wears many different hats in his job.
14. Please table the party until next week.
15. Mike is a Rolodex with his filing system.
16. She is a clock when it comes to telling time.
17. ~~Ireland is a country in Europe.~~
18. Frank is a surgeon with his precision.
19. ~~Mary walked like a soldier down the hall.~~
20. Ciaran is a king with his riches.

Name_____ Date _____

Please write **true** if a metaphor is listed in the sentences below or **false** if a metaphor does not exist.

Example: I am talented when it comes to memorizing poems.   <u>False</u>
         Shelly is a fish in the water when she swims.   <u>True</u>

1. You are my sunshine, my only sunshine.   _____

2. Is Al going to the river to fish next week?   _____

3. How far away is Atlanta, Georgia from Frankfort, Kentucky?   _____

4. You are a rock when it comes to being a good friend.   _____

5. You are a clown in making others laugh.   _____

6. She is so talented with her musical abilities.   _____

7. That gentleman is so strong; he is a mule.   _____

8. I am a vault with my knowledge.   _____

9. The world is a stage and it is all yours.   _____

10. Shannon has the keen eyesight of an owl.   _____

11. Courtney is a giant when she hits the baseball over the fence.   _____

12. The noise is music to my ears.   _____

13. Her heart is gold when it comes to volunteering.   _____

14. Sally walks like a snail whenever she approaches her teacher.   _____

15. The baseball manager said his pitcher is a diamond in the rough.   _____

16. I am in a good mood today.   _____

17. Is Tara really as bright as the sun with her personality?   _____

18. Please don't delay doing your homework because time is a thief.   _____

19. I always feel blue when I lose my wallet.   _____

20. Is she really a statue when it comes to remaining quiet?   _____

ANSWER KEY

1.	You are my sunshine, my only sunshine.	**True**
2.	Is Al going to the river to fish next week?	**False**
3.	How far away is Atlanta, Georgia from Frankfort, Kentucky?	**False**
4.	You are a rock when it comes to being a good friend.	**True**
5.	You are a clown in making others laugh.	**True**
6.	She is so talented with her musical abilities.	**False**
7.	That gentleman is so strong; he is a mule.	**True**
8.	I am a vault with my knowledge.	**True**
9.	The world is a stage and it is all yours.	**True**
10.	Shannon has the keen eyesight of an owl.	**True**
11.	Courtney is a giant when she hits the baseball over the fence.	**True**
12.	The noise is music to my ears.	**True**
13.	Her heart is gold when it comes to volunteering.	**True**
14.	Sally walks like a snail whenever she approaches her teacher.	**True**
15.	The baseball manager said his pitcher is a diamond in the rough.	**True**
16.	I am in a good mood today.	**False**
17.	Is Tara really as bright as the sun with her personality?	**False**
18.	Please don't delay doing your homework because time is a thief.	**True**
19.	I always feel blue when I lose my wallet.	**True**
20.	Is she really a statue when it comes to remaining quiet?	**True**

Name_____   Date _____

Fill in the blank.

dug up	I'm heartbroken	a melting pot	flocked	was a circus
heated argument	a blanket of snow	crocodile tears	delicate flower	feeding frenzy
things are going smoothly	sweet smell of success	leaping with laughter	my father is a rock	planted the seed
he swam in the sea of happiness	his head was spinning	rolling in the dough	glued in their seats	light at the end of the tunnel

1. The manager of the team got into a _____ with the umpire.
2. She _____ some old information that had never been revealed.
3. _____ covered the ski resort.
4. Some people can be a _____ when speaking of loved ones.
5. They _____ to the front of the stage.
6. _____ with the questions during the tiresome interview.
7. Mrs. Applegate _____ that a test was coming up soon.
8. The fish went into a _____ when food was placed in the tank.
9. _____ ever since my great-grandmother passed away.
10. The audience has been _____ waiting for the ending of the movie.
11. The crowd at the circus was _____ during the clown skit.
12. _____ when he found out he got into the college of his dreams.
13. _____ with his stance on feeding the poor.
14. America is _____ with diversity.
15. There is nothing like the _____ when you put your mind to things.
16. Sally said _____ ever since the groups agreed.
17. My little brother always seems to get _____ when he gets in trouble.
18. The Jenks family has been _____ ever since they won the lottery.
19. I can see _____ .
20. It _____ at the arena when the home team won the game in the final minutes.

Answer Key

1. The manager of the team got into a **heated argument** with the umpire.
2. She **dug up some** old information that had never been revealed.
3. A **blanket of snow** covered the ski resort.
4. Some people can be a **delicate flower** when speaking of loved ones.
5. They **flocked** to the front of the stage.
6. **His head was spinning** with the questions during the tiresome interview.
7. Mrs. Applegate **planted the seed** that a test was coming up soon.
8. The fish went into a **feeding frenzy** when food was placed in the tank.
9. **I'm heart-broken** ever since my great-grandmother passed away.
10. The audience has been **glued in their seats** waiting for the ending of the movie.
11. The crowd at the circus was **leaping with laughter** during the clown skit.
12. **He swam in the sea of happiness** when he found out he got into the college of his dreams.
13. **My father is a rock** with his stance on feeding the poor.
14. America is a **melting pot** with diversity.
15. There is nothing like the **sweet smell of success** when you put your mind to things.
16. Sally said **things are going smoothly** ever since the groups agreed.
17. My little brother always seems to get **crocodile tears** when he gets in trouble.
18. The Jenks family has been **rolling in the dough** ever since they won the lottery.
19. I can see **light at the end of the tunnel**.
20. It **was a circus** at the arena when the home team won the game in the final minutes.

Name_____ Date _____

Please fill in the blank spaces to make the metaphors complete sentences. You will need to use your imagination to make the metaphors come to life.

Examples: He is the _____ when he runs.

He is the **wind** when he runs.

1. I am feeling_____ ever since the parade was cancelled.

2. My mom is broken_____ because she lost her diamond ring.

3. There is a_____ of paper on my desk to be graded.

4. My son is the_____ of my eye.

5. Mary is a_____ with her knowledge.

6. Janette is a_____ when it comes to solving math problems.

7. My heart is a_____ because I am so nervous about the speech.

8. I smell something_____ about that story.

9. My cat was a_____ when the barking dog was near.

10. You are a_____ of sunshine every day!

Please write your own metaphors in complete sentences.

1. _____

2. _____

3. _____

4. _____

5. _____

Name_____ Date_____

Please use the following metaphors in complete sentences.

1. (mountain of riches) _____

_____

2. (the room is a pigsty)_____

_____

3. (she is a skyscraper) _____

_____

4. (hugs are medicine) _____

_____

5. (walking encyclopedia) _____

_____

6. (the world is my oyster) _____

_____

7. (sea of grief) _____

_____

8. (light of my life) _____

_____

9. (a turtle when you run) _____

_____

10. (the apple of my eye) _____

_____

Name_____ Date_____

What does each metaphor example mean?
Example: Billy is a mountain of a man.
         This metaphor means Billie is a very big person.

1. Are you fishing for a compliment again?

   _____

2. Mary has had a broken heart ever since her cat Mittens ran away.

   _____

3. Betty's mom told her she is the light of her life.

   _____

4. Does Sally have the bubbliest personality?

   _____

5. I am going to fade off to sleep.

   _____

6. He has the heart of a lion.

   _____

7. You had better pull your socks up because the weather is changing.

   _____

8. Hannah was jumping for joy when her name was called.

   _____

9. There is a mountain of laundry to be completed.

   _____

10. The old pigeon kicked the bucket.

    _____

Name _____ Date_____

Please write a comprehensive paragraph using at least **four metaphors**.

_____

_____

_____

_____

_____

_____

_____

_____

_____

_____

_____

_____

_____

_____

_____

_____

_____

_____

_____

_____

Name_____ Date _____

Please write a sentence using a favorite metaphor. Illustrate that favorite metaphor.

Cumulative Review

Name_____ Date _____

Please circle the appropriate response.

1. I am a vault with my knowledge.
   simile							metaphor						neither

2. Shea is a mammoth with his size.
   simile							metaphor						neither

3. Did you wave to the camera during the snapshot?
   simile							metaphor						neither

4. How far away is New Mexico from Maine?
   simile							metaphor						neither

5. My dog is as clever as a fox.
   simile							metaphor						neither

6. Why is there a mountain of clothes in the laundry basket?
   simile							metaphor						neither

7. The sun is shining today.
   simile							metaphor						neither

8. I am a roller coaster with my emotions lately.
   simile							metaphor						neither

9. My teacher said I am a diamond in the rough.
   simile							metaphor						neither

10. Please don't shout out incorrect answers like an auctioneer!
    simile							metaphor						neither

11. The raft floated downstream like a rocket during the storm.
    simile							metaphor						neither

12. My eyes are as clear as the sky when I am in a great mood.
    simile							metaphor						neither

13. My heart is a blanket of love for my mom.
    simile							metaphor						neither

14. Why does vacation pass as quickly as a cheetah running?
    simile							metaphor						neither

15. Your key to success is being the best possible student you can be.
    simile							metaphor						neither

Answer Key

1. I am a vault with my knowledge.
   simile — **metaphor** — neither

2. Shea is a mammoth with his size.
   simile — **metaphor** — neither

3. Did you wave to the camera during the snapshot?
   simile — metaphor — **neither**

4. How far away is New Mexico from Maine?
   simile — metaphor — **neither**

5. My dog is as clever as a fox.
   simile — metaphor — neither

6. Why is there a mountain of clothes in the laundry basket?
   simile — **metaphor** — neither

7. The sun is shining today.
   simile — metaphor — **neither**

8. I am a roller coaster with my emotions lately.
   simile — **metaphor** — neither

9. My teacher said I am a diamond in the rough.
   simile — **metaphor** — neither

10. Please don't shout out incorrect answers like an auctioneer!
    simile — metaphor — neither

11. The raft floated downstream like a rocket during the storm.
    simile — metaphor — neither

12. My eyes are as clear as the sky when I am in a great mood.
    simile — metaphor — neither

13. My heart is a blanket of love for my mom.
    simile — **metaphor** — neither

14. Why does vacation pass as quickly as a cheetah running?
    simile — metaphor — neither

15. Your key to success is being the best possible student you can be.
    simile — **metaphor** — neither

Name _____ Date _____

Cut apart the simile and metaphor sentences and glue them in the appropriate column.

Simile	Metaphor

It is as cold as an ice cube outside.	I was a rock last night when I slept.
He laughed like a hyena after hearing the joke.	Harry was as happy as a lark when he found his wallet.
Trevor is a king with his riches.	She is a clock when it comes to telling time.
She is a rainbow with her outgoing personality.	CJ ran like the wind during the race.
I was as hot as the sun outside during recess.	Sarah is a butterfly when she is on stage doing ballet.
The noise is music to my ears.	Tara can talk as quickly as an auctioneer when she is excited.
I was as proud as a peacock when I received an A on my report.	I always feel blue when the weekend is over.
I am a vault with secrets.	She was as excited as a puppy to see her new brother.
Tim is as cool as a cucumber when he plays the piano at his recital.	Jim is the light of his mom's life.

Name_____   Date _____

> **Personification-** a figure of speech in which human characteristics are given to an animal or an object
> **Examples:**
> 1. My turtle winked at me when I left the house.
> 2. The grass cried when I ran after the ball.
> 3. The pencil begged to be used during the exam.
> 4. The clouds pushed the sun aside.

Circle the personification examples listed below, and put a line through sentences that don't contain personification.

1. The wind howled across the frigid forest.
2. The sun smiled at me today.
3. A rainstorm washed all the cars in the city.
4. Herman's blanket wrapped itself around my legs.
5. The tulips waved to the other flowers on the farm.
6. How did the sun push its way across the sky?
7. Tommy's cat can crawl so quickly.
8. Sydney's snowman cried when he was melting.
9. The desert is too hot during the summer.
10. Molly's engine roared when she stepped on the accelerator.
11. My heart has been skipping around in my chest since I made honor roll.
12. The flag waved frantically in the wind.
13. My classmates are some of the best people I know.
14. Sally jogged out of the room because she was upset.
15. Maxine ran so fast she fell to the ground.
16. My friend said good-bye to his sister at the airport.
17. The married couple smiled while leaving the church.
18. The grasshopper jumped over the leaf.
19. The book was calling my name.
20. Jessie bounced around the house on his birthday.

Answer Key

1. The **wind howled** across the frigid forest.
2. The **sun smiled** at me today.
3. A **rainstorm washed** all the cars in the city.
4. Herman's **blanket wrapped** itself around my legs.
5. The **tulips waved** to the other flowers on the farm.
6. How did the **sun push** its way across the sky?
7. ~~Tommy's cat can crawl so quickly.~~
8. Sydney's **snowman cried** when he was melting.
9. ~~The desert is too hot during the summer.~~
10. Molly's **engine roared** when she stepped on the accelerator.
11. My **heart has been skipping** around in my chest since I made honor roll.
12. The **flag waved** frantically in the wind.
13. ~~My classmates are some of the best people I know.~~
14. ~~Sally jogged out of the room because she was upset.~~
15. ~~Maxine ran so fast she fell to the ground.~~
16. ~~My friend said good-bye to his sister at the airport.~~
17. ~~The married couple smiled while leaving the church.~~
18. ~~The grasshopper jumped over the leaf.~~
19. The **book was calling** my name.
20. ~~Jessie bounced around the house on his birthday.~~

A Yearlong Guide to Figurative Language

Name_____ Date _____

Please write **true** if personification is located in the sentence below or **false** if personification does not exist.

1. Jack is the only friend that I can count on. _____

2. The cactus pointed to visitors in the desert. _____

3. Pauline skipped across the prairie during spring. _____

4. June politely asked if she could use the school computer. _____

5. Mariah likes taking the bus to school. _____

6. The darkness blanketed the town on Halloween. _____

7. The happy mom smiled at her baby in the nursery. _____

8. Jane heard the last piece of cake in the refrigerator calling her name. _____

9. The sorry engine wheezed its death cough. _____

10. Brian and Tim are going on vacation to Bermuda. _____

11. The buses can be impatient in this town. _____

12. The vending machine ate my money for the second time this week. _____

13. Dane reached for the book and slipped. _____

14. The candle flame danced in the dark. _____

15. I have a folder of work to complete by noon. _____

16. The rain pounded on the windows. _____

17. The sweater I am wearing is quite itchy. _____

18. The grass is always greener on the other side. _____

19. My home country is located in Europe. _____

20. The sunflowers nodded in the wind. _____

Answer Key

1. Jack is the only friend that I can count on. — **False**
2. The cactus pointed to visitors in the desert. — **True**
3. Pauline skipped across the prairie during spring. — **False**
4. June politely asked if she could use the computer. — **False**
5. Mariah likes taking the bus to school. — **False**
6. The darkness blanketed the town on Halloween. — **True**
7. The happy mom smiled at her baby in the nursery. — **False**
8. Jane heard the last piece of cake in the refrigerator calling her name. — **True**
9. The sorry engine wheezed its death cough. — **True**
10. Brian and Tim are going on vacation to Bermuda. — **False**
11. The buses can be impatient in this town. — **True**
12. The vending machine ate my money for the second time this week. — **True**
13. Dane reached for the book and slipped. — **False**
14. The candle flame danced in the dark. — **True**
15. I have a folder of work to complete by noon. — **False**
16. The rain pounded on the windows. — **True**
17. The sweater I am wearing is quite itchy. — **False**
18. The grass is always greener on the other side. — **False**
19. My home country is located in Europe. — **False**
20. The sunflowers nodded in the wind. — **True**

Name _____   Date _____

Personification fill in the blank

ants marched	angry clouds	light sent flashes	rapid's fighting	the fan swirled
ate the grass	turkeys jogged	tilted its branches	sun threw itself	tires screech
the nutcrackers smiled	the cookies crumbled	the porcupine popped balloons	the stapler screamed	oven door got cranky
wind whispered	the water shivered	the turtle groaned	wrapper begged	the thunder clapped

1. The candy bar _____ to be opened.
2. The _____ when I pressed too hard.
3. The _____ when it was left closed all day.
4. I thought I was seeing things when the _____ on Thanksgiving.
5. Many were sad when the _____ threw rain on the parade.
6. The _____ all the way to the picnic.
7. The river's current was so strong; I could have sworn I saw _____ .
8. My sister's lawn mower _____ .
9. The tree _____ during the storm.
10. The _____ as I poured ice into my drink.
11. The _____ before I could reach the last of them.
12. Did the _____ when the truck passed?
13. The _____ on the town for days during the heat wave.
14. During the parade, the _____ and came to life.
15. The _____ so loudly my ears hurt.
16. The _____ when the canoe passed by in the water.
17. While walking down the lane, _____ for me to relax.
18. The _____ during the party in the yard.
19. The _____ and gave us relief during the heat wave.
20. The _____ before it went out.

Answer Key

1. The candy bar **wrapper begged** to be opened.
2. The **stapler screamed** when I pressed too hard.
3. The **oven door got cranky** when it was left closed all day.
4. I thought I was seeing things when the **turkeys jogged** on Thanksgiving.
5. Many were sad when the **angry clouds** threw rain on the parade.
6. The **ants marched** all the way to the picnic.
7. The river's current was so strong; I could have sworn I saw **rapids fighting.**
8. My sister's lawn mower **ate the grass.**
9. The tree **tilted its branches** during the storm.
10. The **water shivered** as I poured ice into my drink.
11. The **cookies crumbled** before I could reach the last of them.
12. Did the **tires screech** when the truck passed?
13. The sun **threw itself** on the town for days during the heat wave.
14. During the parade, the **nutcrackers smiled** and came to life.
15. The **thunder clapped** so loudly my ears hurt.
16. The **turtle groaned** when the canoe passed by in the water.
17. While walking down the lane, the **wind whispered** for me to relax.
18. The **porcupine popped the balloons** during the party in the yard.
19. The **fan swirled** and gave us relief during the heat wave.
20. The **light sent flashes** before it went out.

Name_____ Date_____

Please use the following personification samples in sentences.

1. (the tire screamed) _____
_____

2. (the hyena laughed) _____
_____

3. (a willow trembled) _____
_____

4. (the desert cried) _____
_____

5. (my pencil shook) _____
_____

6. (the painting smiled) _____
_____

7. (the sun raced) _____
_____

8. (the sloth waved) _____
_____

9. (the lark sang) _____
_____

10. (the clock bellowed) _____
_____

Name_____   Date _____

What does each personification example mean?
Example: The misty-eyed eraser sat motionless in the classroom.
         The eraser was sad because nobody used it.

1. The shy guitar waited to be played all day.

   _____

2. My necklace screamed when I took it off.

   _____

3. The polite polar bear strolled across the tundra.

   _____

4. The bashful plant hid behind the tree.

   _____

5. Liam's angry lama walked away.

   _____

6. The hill cried when the children did cartwheels.

   _____

7. The radio sang all week long.

   _____

8. The napkin ran away from the table when I opened the window.

   _____

9. Kelly's mittens wrapped around her hands during the blizzard.

   _____

10. The pumpkin patch complained about the scarecrows.

    _____

Name_____ Date _____

Please write a comprehensive paragraph using at least four personification examples.

Name _____ Date _____

Please write a favorite personification example in a complete sentence. Make an illustration of your personification example.

Name_____ Date _____

> **Hyperbole-** an extreme exaggeration to make a point and the opposite of an "understatement."
> **Examples:**
> 1. I am so hungry I could eat a horse.
> 2. I have told you a million times to stop talking during the play.
> 3. I had a ton of homework.
> 4. My notebook cost eight hundred dollars.

Circle the hyperbole examples listed below and put a line through sentences that do not contain hyperboles.

1. He's got tons of money.
2. Her brain is the size of an ocean.
3. His idea is older than the hills.
4. She ran so fast during the marathon.
5. Tina has so many great ideas.
6. It is so hot outside the sun is scalding me.
7. My father walked uphill to school in the snow for years.
8. My mother danced during her high school reunion.
9. John jumped a hundred times in a row.
10. Shannon laughed so hard at the funny clown.
11. His smile was a mile wide.
12. The crowds boarded the train in Prague.
13. My to-do list is a mile long.
14. The park ranger has been working here forever.
15. Sandra's husband likes walking along the beach.
16. It seems like centuries since I have seen you.
17. Did Phil ever make it to Oregon?
18. The doctor's office had three hundred people in the waiting room.
19. Brent's cousin lives on another planet.
20. I think computers are awesome.

Answer Key

1. **He's got tons of money.**
2. **Her brain is the size of an ocean.**
3. **His idea is older than the hills.**
4. ~~She ran so fast during the marathon.~~
5. ~~Tina has so many great ideas.~~
6. **It is so hot outside the sun is scalding me.**
7. **My father walked uphill to school in the snow for years.**
8. ~~My mother danced during her high school reunion.~~
9. **John jumped a hundred times in a row.**
10. ~~Shannon laughed so hard at the funny clown.~~
11. **His smile was a mile wide.**
12. ~~The crowds boarded the train in Prague.~~
13. **My to-do list is a mile long.**
14. **The park ranger has been working here forever.**
15. ~~Sandra's husband likes walking along the beach.~~
16. **It seems like centuries since I have seen you.**
17. ~~Did Phil ever make it to Oregon?~~
18. **The doctor's office had three hundred people in the waiting room.**
19. **Brent's cousin lives on another planet.**
20. ~~I think computers are awesome.~~

Name_____ Date _____

Please write **true** if hyperbole is located in the sentence below or **false** if hyperbole does not exist.

1. Brenda can run at the speed of light. _____

2. The farmhouse is across from the pond. _____

3. I was so embarrassed I thought I might die. _____

4. I am so exhausted I could sleep all week. _____

5. Patrick's leg is swollen from the bee sting. _____

6. Miss Grimsby walked into the room with my cousin. _____

7. My mom told me to stop talking a mile a minute. _____

8. Is that turtle running 50 mph? _____

9. That giraffe is so small I can barely see him. _____

10. Mr. Biggs is the size of a mountain. _____

11. Her smile lights up the whole entire county. _____

12. The puddle is the size of a lake. _____

13. How far away is the auditorium from here? _____

14. My car is older than dirt. _____

15. There were at least a million cartoons on television this weekend. _____

16. The Earth spins on its axis. _____

17. There are fifty states in the US. _____

18. The elephant is bigger than Mars. _____

19. Jennifer hit the softball to the next town. _____

20. My baseball team won three hundred games in a row. _____

Answer Key

1. Brenda can run at the speed of light. — **True**
2. The farmhouse is across from the pond. — **False**
3. I was so embarrassed I thought I might die. — **True**
4. I am so exhausted I could sleep all week. — **True**
5. Patrick's leg is swollen from the bee sting. — **False**
6. Miss Grimsby walked into the room with my cousin. — **False**
7. My mom told me to stop talking a mile a minute. — **True**
8. Is that turtle running 50 mph? — **True**
9. That giraffe is so small I can barely see him. — **True**
10. Mr. Biggs is the size of a mountain. — **True**
11. Her smile lights up the whole entire county. — **True**
12. The puddle is the size of a lake. — **True**
13. How far away is the auditorium from here? — **False**
14. My car is older than dirt. — **True**
15. There were at least a million cartoons on television this weekend. — **True**
16. The Earth spins on its axis. — **False**
17. There are fifty states in the US. — **False**
18. The elephant is bigger than Mars. — **True**
19. Jennifer hit the softball to the next town. — **True**
20. My baseball team won three hundred games in a row. — **True**

Name _____   Date _____

Hyperbole fill in the blank

I nearly died	pizzas up to the ceiling	a mountain of riches	a million kittens	the clown told fifty jokes in a row
I ate the whole thing	line is a mile long	don't take all day	everybody ran for miles	Joe made 345 jump shots during recess
have a melt down	it landed on the moon	I spent all day at the mall	loves her to Saturn	the most homework in the world
laughed for weeks	penguins were wearing scarves	I was lost for days	juggle fifty batons	Phil breaking a thousand pencils during the test

1. It was so cold outside today that even the _____.
2. I can't believe _____ when nobody thought I could finish.
3. John _____ when he heard the funny joke.
4. The laundry pile was so messy _____.
5. I was wondering what sound I could hear but it was _____.
6. He is so talented that he can _____ at once.
7. Mrs. Smith told her daughter she _____ and back.
8. James arrived at the giveaway late and now the _____.
9. Why is it I always end up in the class that gets _____?
10. The pizzeria made _____ for our party.
11. She came upon _____ when she struck gold.
12. _____ chased the yarn in the yard.
13. _____, and I still couldn't buy anything.
14. Alicia hit the ball so far _____.
15. When the hippo came out of the river, _____.
16. Please _____ making a decision if you want ice cream.
17. While I was at the carnival, _____.
18. _____ when I heard Jill placed first.
19. An all time school record was set when _____.
20. Please don't _____ if Cindy moves to Michigan.

Answer Key

1. It was so cold outside today that even the **penguins were wearing scarves**.
2. I can't believe **I ate the whole thing** when nobody thought I could finish.
3. John **laughed for weeks** when he heard the funny joke.
4. The laundry pile was so messy **I was lost for days**.
5. I was wondering what sound I could hear but it was **Phil breaking a thousand pencils during the test**.
6. He is so talented that he can **juggle fifty batons** at once.
7. Mrs. Smith told her daughter she **loves her to Saturn** and back.
8. James arrived at the giveaway late and now the **line is a mile long**.
9. Why is it I always end up in the class that gets **the most homework in the world**?
10. The pizzeria made **pizzas up to the ceiling** for our party.
11. She came upon **a mountain of riches** when she struck gold.
12. **A million kittens** chased the yarn in the yard.
13. **I spent all day at the mall**, and I still couldn't buy anything.
14. Alicia hit the ball so far **it landed on the moon**.
15. When the hippo came out of the river, **everybody ran for miles**.
16. Please **don't take all day** making a decision if you want ice cream.
17. While I was at the carnival, **the clown told fifty jokes in a row**.
18. **I nearly died** when I heard Jill place first.
19. An all time school record was set when **Joe made 345 jump shots during recess**.
20. Please don't **have a meltdown** if Cindy moves to Michigan.

Name_____ Date _____

Please use the following hyperbole samples in sentences.

1. (bigger than a house) _____
_____

2. (an ocean of tears) _____
_____

3. (a Grand Canyon of a heart) _____
_____

4. (a million times) _____
_____

5. (I've waited for Ice Ages) _____
_____

6. (colder than ice)_____
_____

7. (the loudest roar ever) _____
_____

8. (our teacher yells all day) _____
_____

9. (the fire ant bit sixty people) _____
_____

10. (all over the news)_____
_____

Name _____   Date _____

What does each hyperbole example mean?
Example: Stop crying wolf all day when you don't need help.
         Stop asking for assistance when you don't need any.

1. I am so hungry I could eat a million apples.
_____

2. The mosquito was bigger than an airplane.
_____

3. I had to walk 15 miles to school in the sleet.
_____

4. I'm so busy trying to accomplish ten million things at once.
_____

5. I have homework that will take weeks to complete.
_____

6. I will die if she asks me to sing in front of everyone.
_____

7. The whole world is staring at me.
_____

8. I could walk across the Earth faster than you eat your cookies.
_____

9. His teeth were blinding white.
_____

10. The desert was hotter than the sun.
_____

Name _____   Date _____

Please write a comprehensive paragraph using at least four hyperbole examples.

Name_____ Date _____

Please use hyperbole in a complete sentence. Make an illustration of your hyperbole example.

Name_____   Date _____

> **Idiom:** a set expression of two or more words that means something other than the literal meanings of its individual words.
> **Examples:**
> 1. Please cough up the information.
> 2. I smell something fishy going on around here.
> 3. My goldfish kicked the bucket last week.
> 4. Is there a frog in your throat?

Circle the idiom examples listed below and put a line through sentences that do not contain idioms

1. Are you pulling my leg by saying George Washington is a distant relative?
2. I don't know how I am going to make ends meet this month.
3. Somebody needs to step up, and take the bull by its horns.
4. My house has so many rooms.
5. We're not out of the woods yet with the situation we are in.
6. Your grade is on the line if you don't study for the test.
7. She got in so much trouble for sleeping late.
8. Don't be a wet blanket when it comes to having fun.
9. I know you are excited about the carnival, but please don't drive me up the wall about going.
10. Marty makes me laugh when he tells all his jokes.
11. She is such a crack up.
12. Sue makes lemonade every day of the week.
13. Mary can make a mountain out of a molehill with everything.
14. Nancy studies every single night.
15. Are you out in left field today?
16. Did you wake up on the wrong side of the bed?
17. Does the cat have your tongue all of a sudden?
18. I am going to the circus next week with my family.
19. I feel all boxed in.
20. Maya skipped across the playground.

Answer Key

1. Are you pulling my leg by saying George Washington is a distant relative?
2. I don't know how I am going to make ends meet this month.
3. Somebody needs to step up, and take the bull by its horns.
4. ~~My house has so many rooms.~~
5. We're not out of the woods yet with the situation we are in.
6. Your grade is on the line if you don't study for the test.
7. ~~She got in so much trouble for sleeping late.~~
8. Don't be a wet blanket when it comes to having fun.
9. I know you are excited about the carnival, but please don't drive me up the wall about going.
10. ~~Marty makes me laugh when he tells all his jokes.~~
11. She is such a crack up.
12. ~~Sue makes lemonade every day of the week.~~
13. Mary can make a mountain out of a molehill with everything.
14. ~~Nancy studies every single night.~~
15. Are you out in left field today?
16. Did you wake up on the wrong side of the bed?
17. Does the cat have your tongue all of a sudden?
18. ~~I am going to the circus next week with my family.~~
19. I feel all boxed in.
20. ~~Maya skipped across the playground.~~

A Yearlong Guide to Figurative Language

Name_____ Date _____

Please write **true** if an idiom is located in the sentence below, or **false** if an idiom does not exist.

1. My uncle is a great mechanic. _____

2. Where can I find an alternate route for the parade? _____

3. Actions speak louder than words. _____

4. I have knots in my stomach. _____

5. The bees buzzed around the hive. _____

6. You need to act your age in the museum. _____

7. Do you have ants in your pants today because of the trip? _____

8. I know you might be down, but when one door shuts, another opens. _____

9. She can dance really well for just learning the routine. _____

10. The cheerleaders made the crowd get up and scream. _____

11. You can lead a horse to water. _____

12. When the going gets tough, the tough get going. _____

13. I broke my sister's bike and now she is mad at me. _____

14. The substitute had good manners. _____

15. Why did you let the cat out of the bag? _____

16. Did Minnie really tell me to break a leg at the ski lodge? _____

17. We are up against the clock and need to finish soon. _____

18. Jason has a green thumb. _____

19. My mom made lots of cupcakes for the celebration. _____

20. A little bird told me you haven't finished your work. _____

Answer Key

1.	My uncle is a great mechanic.	**False**
2.	Where can I find an alternate route for the parade?	**False**
3.	Actions speak louder than words.	**True**
4.	I have knots in my stomach.	**True**
5.	The bees buzzed around the hive.	**False**
6.	You need to act your age in the museum.	**True**
7.	Do you have ants in your pants today because of the trip?	**True**
8.	I know you might be down, but when one door shuts, another opens.	**True**
9.	She can dance really well for just learning the routine.	**False**
10.	The cheerleaders made the crowd get up and scream.	**False**
11.	You can lead a horse to water.	**False**
12.	When the going gets tough, the tough get going.	**True**
13.	I broke my sister's bike and now she is mad at me.	**False**
14.	The substitute had good manners.	**False**
15.	Why did you let the cat out of the bag?	**True**
16.	Did Minnie really tell me to break a leg at the ski lodge?	**True**
17.	We are up against the clock and need to finish soon.	**True**
18.	Jason has a green thumb.	**True**
19.	My mom made lots of cupcakes for the celebration.	**False**
20.	A little bird told me you haven't finished your work.	**True**

Name_____   Date _____

Idiom fill in the blank

hang on	stop on a dime	bug eyes	over the moon	hit the road
talk is cheap	heart of a lion	apple of my eye	all walks of life	table talk
all in a day's work	my mind's made up	all bark and no bite	the best of both worlds	lump in her throat
feeling a bit under the weather	a wolf in sheep's clothing	phone rang off the hook	early bird got the worm	I got lost in my thoughts

1. Don't fear the puppy, she is _____ .
2. Ethel is the _____ .
3. Please _____, and I will be right with you.
4. While the robin slept, the _____ .
5. _____ Jack, and please don't come back.
6. That's final, _____ .
7. If you go to the fair, you will see _____ .
8. Due to the sudden rain, I am _____ .
9. My sister's _____ when she won the lottery.
10. _____, and daydreamed for hours.
11. My mom said, _____ .
12. He can _____ while ice-skating.
13. I am _____ with excitement.
14. Janice had a _____ giving the speech.
15. You have _____ by speaking two languages fluently.
16. _____, and your actions speak much more.
17. The fox is _____ .
18. I had _____ when the noise scared me.
19. Please don't use _____ in front of company.
20. My dad has the _____ with his generosity.

Answer Key

1. Don't fear the puppy, she is all bark and no bite.
2. Ethel is the apple of my eye.
3. Please hang on, and I will be right with you.
4. While the robin slept, the early bird got the worm.
5. Hit the road Jack, and please don't come back.
6. That's final, my mind is made up.
7. If you go to the fair, you will see all walks of life.
8. Due to the sudden rain, I am feeling a bit under the weather.
9. My sister's phone rang off the hook when she won the lottery.
10. I got lost in my thoughts, and daydreamed for hours.
11. My mom said, "It's all in a day's work."
12. He can stop on a dime while ice-skating.
13. I am over the moon with excitement.
14. Janice had a lump in her throat giving the speech.
15. You have the best of both worlds by speaking two languages fluently.
16. Talk is cheap, and your actions speak much more.
17. The fox is a wolf in sheep's clothing.
18. I had bug eyes when the noise scared me.
19. Please don't use table talk in front of company.
20. My dad has the heart of a lion with his generosity.

Name_____ Date _____

Please use the following idiom samples in sentences.

1. (out of the woods) _____
_____

2. (play it by ear) _____
_____

3. (butterflies in my stomach) _____
_____

4. (skating on thin ice)_____
_____

5. (the early bird gets the worm)_____
_____

6. (to hear something straight from the horse's mouth) _____
_____

7. (costs an arm and a leg) _____
_____

8. (the last straw) _____
_____

9. (take what someone says with a grain of salt) _____
_____

10. (sit on the fence)_____
_____

Name_____   Date _____

What does each idiom mean?
Example: Please cough up the information.
         Pleas give up the information.

1. A penny for your thoughts is all it costs.

   _____

2. Please don't add insult to injury after the loss.

   _____

3. That is one hot potato of a topic.

   _____

4. Once in a blue moon you will see a killer whale.

   _____

5. We don't see eye to eye on this subject matter.

   _____

6. Did I hear it through the grapevine that you became a doctor?

   _____

7. Don't miss the boat with this golden opportunity.

   _____

8. You can kill two birds with one stone if you bring your lunch and games to the picnic.

   _____

9. Are you on the ball today?

   _____

10. Please don't cut corners while studying.

    _____

Name_____ Date _____

Please write a comprehensive paragraph using at least four idioms.

Name_____ Date _____

Please use an idiom in a complete sentence. Make an illustration of your idiom example.

A Yearlong Guide to Figurative Language

Name_____   Date _____

Please circle the appropriate response.

1. Carl candidly called the radio station and won the contest.
   idiom   hyperbole   personification   other

2. It really gets my goat when my car stalls.
   idiom   hyperbole   personification   other

3. Mrs. Johnson is the most down-to-earth person.
   idiom   hyperbole   personification   other

4. Shy Sal slid across the stage during the play.
   idiom   hyperbole   personification   other

5. The lightning danced across the night sky.
   idiom   hyperbole   personification   other

6. Larry's loud laugh needs to be lowered.
   idiom   hyperbole   personification   other

7. Why is your scarf longer than a giraffe's neck?
   idiom   hyperbole   personification   other

8. Did your aunt really sled down Mount Everest?
   idiom   hyperbole   personification   other

9. The winds pushed the kite across the sky.
   idiom   hyperbole   personification   other

10. My computer is able to crunch numbers on its own.
    idiom   hyperbole   personification   other

11. I have been told I am a jack-of-all-trades.
    idiom   hyperbole   personification   other

12. My dad's racecar goes faster than the sped of light.
    idiom   hyperbole   personification   other

Answer Key

Answers have been marked in bold.

1. Carl candidly called the radio station and won the contest.
   idiom   hyperbole   personification   **other**

2. It really gets my goat when my car stalls.
   idiom   hyperbole   personification   other

3. Mrs. Johnson is the most down-to-earth person.
   idiom   hyperbole   personification   other

4. Shy Sal slid across the stage during the play.
   idiom   hyperbole   personification   **other**

5. The lightning danced across the night sky.
   idiom   hyperbole   **personification**   other

6. Larry's loud laugh needs to be lowered.
   idiom   hyperbole   personification   **other**

7. 7. Why is your scarf longer than a giraffe's neck?
   idiom   **hyperbole**   personification   other

8. Did your aunt really sled down Mount Everest?
   idiom   **hyperbole**   personification   other

9. The winds pushed the kite across the sky.
   idiom   hyperbole   **personification**   other

10. My computer is able to crunch numbers on its own.
    idiom   hyperbole   **personification**   other

11. I have been told I am a jack-of-all-trades.
    idiom   hyperbole   personification   other

12. My dad's racecar goes faster than the sped of light.
    idiom   **hyperbole**   personification   other

Made in the USA
San Bernardino, CA
29 February 2016